VANCOUVER ISLAND *Vs* THE WORLD

Born and raised on Vancouver Island, I have always regarded "my Island" as one of the most beautiful places on this planet. Despite this love, my passion is to travel and I have been lucky enough to visit over 75 countries, so far.

In 2008 I visited 50 countries, in 50 weeks, interviewed women in their 50s and then chronicled my adventure in my last book entitled *50ish*.

The idea for this photo essay, *Vancouver Island Vs the World,* came as I ventured from country to country and recognized the similarities "my Island" had to many places I was exploring.

This book is intended for both visitors to, and residents of the Island. It is my sincere hope that the reader will enjoy these comparisons as much as I have enjoyed putting them together, and will use it to fully appreciate the stunning beauty Vancouver Island has to offer.

Sincerely

Donna Marie Lynch
Summer 2012

VANCOUVER ISLAND Vs THE WORLD

MANY THANKS TO:

MR. RIGHT FOR HIS LOVE AND HELP IN EDITING

JOHANNA SOCHA FOR HER ADVICE AND EXPERTISE IN GRAPHIC DESIGN.
Island Gals Media Group (www.islandgals.ca)

OTHER BOOKS BY DONNA LYNCH:

50ISH - A JOURNEY TO 50 COUNTRIES IN 50 WEEKS,
INTERVIEWING WOMEN IN THEIR 50S.

www.50ishthebook.com

Library and Archives
Canada Cataloguing in Publication

ISBN 978-0-9867019-1-7

Photography: Donna Marie Lynch

Published by: DML PUBLISHING

Printed in Canada

FSC
www.fsc.org

MIX
Paper from
responsible sources
FSC® C016245

VANCOUVER
ISLAND
Vs
THE WORLD

CAPE SCOTT

PACIFIC
OCEAN

BRITISH
COLUMBIA

COMOX VALLEY

TOFINO   HORNE LAKE   HORNBY

PARKSVILLE

NANAIMO

VANCOUVER

CHEMAINUS

COWICHAN VALLEY/MILL BAY

GOLDSTREAM/MALAHAT

SOOKE   VICTORIA

MT. BAKER

SALISH SEA

USA

PORT
ANGELES

OLYMPIC
MOUNTAINS

SEATTLE

Vancouver Island Fun Facts:

Size
460 Km (290Mi) long / 100Km (60Mi) at widest point
32,262 square kilometers (12,456 square miles)

Population
760,000

Density
24 per square kilometer (62 per square mile)

Highest peak
Golden Hinde - 2,195 meters (7,201 ft)

Largest Pacific island
East of New Zealand

43rd largest island
In the world

Home to Kwakwaka'wakw, Nuu-chah-nulth and Coast Salish people
For thousands of years

After the Europeans arrived in 1774
The Island was named "Quadra and Vancouver Island" after Spanish Captain Juan Franciso de la Bodega y Quadra and British Captain George Vancouver settled on the Island. As the influence of the Spanish waned, during the 1800s, so did the "Quadra" part of the name.

Canada's narrowest street
Fan Tan Alley - Chinatown, Victoria

Canada's oldest Chinatown
Victoria

Canada's tallest waterfall at 440 meters (1,452 ft)
Della Falls, Strathcona Provincial Park

Two UNESCO biosphere reserves
Clayoquot and Arrowsmith

- **Thirty-three species of land mammals**

- **Over 100 Provincial Parks (including Marine Parks)**

- **Over 200 migratory birds**

- **Over 1,000 caves**

- **Over 2,800 farms**

- **Over 9,000 lakes**

VANCOUVER
ISLAND
Vs
THE WORLD

VANCOUVER ISLAND Vs THE WORLD

Manmade Wonders

TOTEMS
U.S.A.	VICTORIA	57

SANDCASTLES
MEXICO	PARKSVILLE	58-59

SPHINXES
EGYPT	VICTORIA	60-61

MURALS
NORTHERN IRELAND	CHEMAINUS	62-63
BRITISH VIRGIN ISLANDS	VICTORIA	64-65

ROCK ART
SOUTH AFRICA	SOOKE	66

Outdoor Adventures

CAVING
CUBA	HORNE LAKE	67

GOLFING
SCOTLAND	VICTORIA	68-69

SURFING
COSTA RICA	TOFINO	70-71

SAILING
AUSTRALIA	VICTORIA	72-73

KAYAKING
NICARAGUA	SALISH SEA	74-75

SKIING
SWITZERLAND	COMOX	76-77

ZIPLINING
ANTIGUA	VICTORIA	78-79

KITESURFING
U.S.A.	VICTORIA	80-81

HIKING
PERU	TOFINO	82-83

Animals

DOLPHINS
NEW ZEALAND	NORTH ISLAND	84-85

RACCOONS
BRAZIL	VICTORIA	86

GREAT BLUE HERONS
COSTA RICA	VICTORIA	87

BLACK BEARS
LAOS	NORTH ISLAND	88

BIG CATS
TANZANIA	NORTH ISLAND	89

LLAMAS
BOLIVIA	VICTORIA	90-91

DEER
NAMIBIA	VICTORIA	92-93

ORCAS
NORWAY	SALISH SEA	94-95

Narrow passes through uninhabited islands, the fjords along the western coast of Chile to the southernmost tip of South America at Cape Horn create a breathtaking cruise and a photographers dream.

CHILEAN FJORDS
CHILE

MALAHAT
VICTORIA

The rolling hills of the Malahat, between Goldstream and Mill Bay, made a route through them an engineering challenge, once thought impossible. However in 1903, a determined Major J.F. McFarlane completed his own survey to prove it could be done. Today this drive with stunning views of the Saanich Peninsula, the Gulf Islands and beyond is one of the most scenic drives on the Island.

The 2,400 kilometers (1,500 miles) of the Himalayas cross mainly in Nepal, Bhutan and India, with outlying parts in Tibet and Pakistan. With more than 100 peaks over 7,200 meters (23,622 ft), this area is a mountain climber's paradise.

HIMALAYAS
NEPAL AND BHUTAN

OLYMPIC MOUNTAINS
WASHINGTON STATE, U.S.A.

They may not be as high as the Himalayas, at 2,427 meters (7,962 ft) at the highest peak, but the impressive mountains on the Olympic Peninsula in Washington State create a glorious year-round, snow peaked mountain backdrop to the city of Victoria.

The most populous of the seven Canary Islands, (Population - 908,000), Tenerife is about 1/15 the size of Vancouver Island (Population - 760,000). Spectacular coastlines surround the island.

Tenerife
CANARY ISLANDS, SPAIN

BEACHES OF PARKSVILLE
PARKSVILLE

Tides that go out seemingly forever, leaving tidal pools, warm ocean water and dramatic rocky coastlines have made Parksville, on the protected east side of Vancouver Island, a popular vacation spot.

This volcano in the Chilean Andes is 2,652 meters (8,701ft) high. The town of Puerto Montt is towered by this beautiful snow peaked mountain. The last eruption was in 1869.

OSORNO VOLCANO
PUERTO MONTT, CHILE

MOUNT BAKER
WASHINGTON STATE, U.S.A.

Seen from the Southeast side of Vancouver Island Mt. Baker, in the Cascade Mountains of Washington State, at 3,286 meters (10,791 ft.) looms so near, the skiers sliding down the mountain can almost be seen on clear sunny winter days.

D escending Dragon Bay is a UNESCO World Heritage Site. Close to 2,000 limestone Isles of various sizes and shapes grace this incredible bay.

HALONG BAY
VIETNAM

Barkley Sound
NEAR PACIFIC RIM NATIONAL PARK

Barkley Sound, on Vancouver Island's "wild west coast" is near the Pacific Rim National Park. The area, in an old-growth temperate rainforest, features long sandy beaches for beach combing and strolling, fantastic hiking, surfing, kayaking, wildlife and bird watching, camping and storm watching.

The northern tip of Ireland provides surprisingly tropical beige sand beaches. The water, however, is closer in temperatures to those in Canada than in the tropics.

INISHOWEN PENINSULA
IRELAND

GUISE BAY
CAPE SCOTT

Cape Scott, on the northwest tip of Vancouver Island, is only accessible by boat, or a rugged 24 kilometer hike. White sand beaches, old growth forest, abundant wildlife and remnants of an abandoned Danish settlement make the hike worth every soggy step.

Many beautiful harbours are found around St. John, one of the many Caribbean Islands.

ST. JOHN
U.S. VIRGIN ISLAND

NANAIMO HARBOUR
NANAIMO

Nanaimo's harbour boasts not only moorage and beautiful views, but a dockside shopping area, floating restaurants, walking paths and an inlet for racing remote control boats.

The capital of Finland, Helsinki is surrounded by the sea. Harbour tours around the islands in the Gulf of Finland are very similar to those around Vancouver Island.

INNER HARBOUR
HELSINKI, FINLAND

INNER HARBOUR
VICTORIA

A seaplane port, a busy ferry terminal, a marina, entertaining buskers, world class restaurants, a causeway, First Nations totem poles, the magnificent Fairmont Empress Hotel, the B.C. Parliament Buildings and the CPR Steamship Building make Victoria's downtown Inner Harbour a year-round place to be.

Turkey is known for its considerable archeological history that can fill weeks of exploration. It also has many beautiful natural sights. This waterfall is just one of them.

WATERFALL
TURKEY

COURTENAY RIVER
COMOX VALLEY

The Tsolum River and the Puntledge River merge to become the Courtenay River which runs through Courtenay in the Comox Valley. In the summer months, the river is lovely for swimming.

The island of Bali in Indonesia has many beautiful waterfalls, usually found only after hiking a rugged trail and passing many Hindu statues and monuments.

WATERFALL
BALI, INDONESIA

One of many waterfalls found on Vancouver Island, Little Niagara Falls is found only steps away from the highway in Goldstream Park on the Malahat Drive. This park has great hiking trails through the tall old-growth forest. There are campgrounds and many picnic sites along the stream. Thousands of spawning salmon can be seen in the fall.

LITTLE NIAGARA FALLS
VICTORIA

The Atacama Desert is the driest desert in the world. Many unique rock formations, stunning sand dunes and salt lakes cover the 105,000 square kilometer (40,600 square mile) desert.

ATACAMA DESERT
BOLIVIA

Hornby Island, just off the East coast of Vancouver Island, has many beautiful beaches. Tribune Bay, often called "Little Hawaii" is the best. Along with white sandy beaches are unusual sandstone rock formations easily accessible to explore.

TRIBUNE BAY
HORNBY ISLAND

This tree was planted in Plaza Francia in 1878, facing the Recoleta Cemetery. Its tentacle-like branches reach out over 50 meters (164 ft).

GRAN GOMERO (RUBBER TREE)
BUENOS AIRES, ARGENTINA

JUAN DE FUCA TRAIL
JUAN DE FUCA PROVINCIAL PARK

Many of the trees in Vancouver Island's old-growth forests have been estimated at over 800 years old and have been measured at over 90 meters (295 ft) tall and 20 meters (65.5ft) in circumference.

MEARES ISLAND
NEAR TOFINO

As much of Vancouver Island is located in a temperate rainforest, so is the area of Los Lagos in Chile. The similarities are endless from picturesque farmland to lakes, rivers and coastlines.

LOS LAGOS REGION
CHILE

Cowichan Valley
COWICHAN

The fertile farmland of the Cowichan Valley makes for a wonderful scenic drive along country roads. Stops at farm markets, wineries, golf courses and coastal villages for fishing, kayaking or a tasty lunch promise days of fulfilling exploration.

Italy has some of the oldest vineyards in the world and is second only to France in producing wine. Italians lead the world in wine consumption.

VINEYARD
TUSCANY, ITALY

VINEYARD
COWICHAN VALLEY

Vancouver Island and the Gulf Islands now have over 40 wineries. An island wine-tasting adventure is a fun way to spend a weekend. Many award winning vintages can be found and several wineries have restaurants or picnic areas where cuisine from local farms can be enjoyed.

Cherry and plum trees blossom throughout Japan. Hanami (meaning "viewing flowers") is an important Japanese custom.

CHERRY BLOSSOMS
JAPAN

BEACON HILL PARK
VICTORIA

In 1930 the City of Victoria imported Japanese cherry trees to plant along the boulevards of many city streets and in Beacon Hill Park. This 62 acre park is home to an animal petting farm, beautiful gardens and trails, picnic areas, a children's playground and wading pool, a small lake and a band pavilion for summer entertainment.

The chateau district around Tours in central France has many wonderful chateaus and castles to visit. Most include intricate gardens and topiary.

TOURS
FRANCE

THE BUTCHART GARDENS
VICTORIA

This spectacular 55 acre garden began with an idea by Jennie Butchart in 1904 to reclaim an old limestone quarry. Now a world renowned attraction and a National Historic Site of Canada, the year-round garden, still owned by family descendants, has summer entertainment, Saturday night fireworks shows, evening illuminations and the magic of Christmas creations which attract locals and visitors alike.

The heavy scent of lavender fills the air on a summer drive through Provence in France. The fields of lavender seem to go on forever.

LAVENDER FARMS
PROVENCE, FRANCE

LAVENDER FARMS
COBBLE HILL

Many lavender farms have popped up on Vancouver Island over the last few years. Most provide tours, picnicking and of course lavender products. One even has a winery! A great way to spend an afternoon.

Also known as the "Palace of Peace and Harmony Lama Temple," these gates provide the entrance to the temple and monastery of the Geluk School of Tibetan Buddhism in Beijing.

THE YONGHEGONG LAMA TEMPLE
BEIJING, CHINA

THE GATE OF HARMONIOUS INTEREST (TONG JI MEN)
VICTORIA

Built in China and erected over Fisgard Street in Victoria in 1981, these gates provide an appealing entrance to Canada's oldest Chinatown, first occupied in 1858. Now a mix of Chinese markets, restaurants, condos and shops.

H onenschwangua Castle, the childhood home of King Ludwig II of Bavaria was built in 1837. As an adult he built Neuschwanstein Castle, which is known as the "Fairytale Castle".

HOHENSCHWANGAU CASTLE
FUSSEN, GERMANY

HATLEY CASTLE
VICTORIA

The castle was commissioned to architect Samuel McClure by James Dunsmuir, son of Robert Dunsmuir, for his family home and was completed in 1908. The family lived there until 1937. It then became a Royal Military College and is now home to Royal Roads University.

This Doric temple was completed in 415 BC. Hephaestus was the patron god of metal working and craftsmanship.

THE TEMPLE OF HEPHAESTUS
ATHENS, GREECE

The Temple of Baal was built in the 1st century AD. It was considered the most important religious building in the Middle East at that time.

THE TEMPLE OF BAAL
PALMYRA, SYRIA

CPR STEAMSHIP TERMINAL
VICTORIA

In 1924 architects P.L. James and Francis Rattenbury designed this impressive building intended to reflect a temple of Poseidon, the Greek God of the sea. Now owned by the Provincial Capital Commission.

W hen arriving in Budapest by boat along the Danube River, the Parliament Buildings on the Pest side of the city makes a remarkable impression. Completed in 1904, the building includes 10 courtyards and 691 rooms.

HUNGARIAN PARLIAMENT BUILDINGS
BUDAPEST, HUNGARY

British Columbia Parliament Buildings
VICTORIA

Twenty-five year old Francis Rattenbury designed these buildings, which officially opened in 1898, but was not completed until 1915. Sitting on the banks of Victoria's Inner Harbour, the buildings are an impressive site, especially at night when they light up with 3,300 lights. Guided tours are offered year round.

Started in 1913, but not completed until 1930 due to WWI, this beautiful Romanesque style cathedral sits in Dom Square in Szeged. Magnificent frescos and mosaics adorn the interior of the church.

VOTIVE CHURCH OF OUR LADY OF HUNGARY
SZEGED, HUNGARY

CRAIGDARROCH CASTLE
VICTORIA

Scottish immigrant, Robert Dunsmuir, who made his fortune from Vancouver Island coal, had the castle built for his family home. Started in 1887, it was completed in 1890, shortly after his death. The Romanesque architecture is seen throughout the building. Tours are offered daily.

Many houseboats line the shores of the canals in Amsterdam. Some are private homes, but many are used for tourist accommodation.

HOUSEBOATS
AMSTERDAM, NETHERLANDS

FISHERMAN'S WHARF
VICTORIA

The houseboats are privately owned, however Fisherman's Wharf offers food kiosks, shops and whale watching tours. It is also a place to buy fresh seafood and if lucky, feed a local seal.

O ld San Juan has over 400 restored buildings from the 16th and 17th-century Spanish colonial period.

Old San Juan
SAN JUAN, PUERTO RICO

LOWER JOHNSON STREET (LO-JO)
VICTORIA, BC

Colourful heritage buildings, some dating back to the 1850s, line the LoJo shopping district in Old Town Victoria. Many independently owned restaurants and fashion boutiques line the street.

I n the East Neuk of Fife, Pittenweem is a quaint fishing village, famous for its fish markets and annual Summer Arts Festival.

PITTENWEEM
SCOTLAND

WHARF STREET
VICTORIA

Originally developed during the gold rush years in the 1850s, Wharf Street on Victoria's downtown harbour offers historical stops, restaurants, shops and marinas.

The city on the Adriatic Sea has been named a UNESCO World Heritage Site. There are many narrow streets and alleys throughout the city.

DUBROVNIC
CROATIA

The narrow streets of the city are spellbinding and getting lost is a definite possibility.

MARRAKESH
MOROCCO

Fan Tan Alley is the narrowest street in Canada. Small shops, a barber, a cafe and an art gallery line the alley.

FAN TAN ALLEY, CHINATOWN
VICTORIA

A large collection of Native American totem poles are found here. This pole with Abe Lincoln on top is a commemorative pole marking the signing of a peace pact between two Tlingit Tribes. The US Cutter Ship - "Lincoln" was instrumental in this, but the figure on the top of a pole must be an animate object.

SAXMAN NATIVE VILLAGE
KETCHIKAN, ALASKA U.S.A

One of the tallest totem poles in the world, at 38.7 meters (127ft-7 inches), was carved by Mungo Martin, David Martin and Henry Hunt, completed in 1954. It is one of many totem poles found throughout the Island that represent the Island's First Nations culture.

KWAKWAKA'WAKW TOTEM
BEACON HILL PARK, VICTORIA

The sand sculptures found on the main beach along the Malecon are created throughout the high season. The sculptors create these intricate forms to collect tips.

SAND SCULPTURE - MALECON
MALECON, PUERTO VALLARTA, MEXICO

SAND SCULPTURE
PARKSVILLE

This limestone statue is thought to have been built by the ancient Egyptians between 2558-2532 BC. It is 73.5 metres (241 ft) long and 6 meters (20 ft) wide.

THE GREAT SPHINX OF GIZA
CAIRO, EGYPT

GALEY FARMS
VICTORIA

Although this replica of the Great Sphinx is 1/2 scale and built about 4,000 years later in 2004, it strikes a remarkable resemblance to the original. Galey Farms is a working farm, but also has a corn maze, market and a small railway.

Murals depicting the history and culture of Northern Ireland are scattered on buildings throughout the city of Belfast. Bobby Sands was a volunteer of the Provisional Irish Republican Army and a member of British Parliament who died while on a hunger strike in prison.

MURAL OF BOBBY SANDS
BELFAST, NORTHERN IRELAND

THE LITTLE TOWN THAT DID
CHEMAINUS

This mural "Native Heritage," is one of more than 40 murals painted on walls throughout Chemanius. The murals depict the heritage and culture of this small mid-island community and were painted by local artists as a way to revitalize the town when the local mill was slated to be closed down in the early 80s.

In 1981 a local artist decided to paint this retaining wall. Over 18 meters (60 ft) long, this mural tells the story of the history, tradition and industry of the British Virgin Islands.

Fahie Mural
TORTOLA, BRITISH VIRGIN ISLANDS

THE UNITY WALL
VICTORIA

This concrete breakwater was completed in 1918 and is 850 meters (2,788 ft) long. In 2009 the Greater Victoria Harbour Authority sponsored First Nation Artists to create the Land and Sea Mural. This captivating mural depicts the traditions and history of the Coast Salish Nations.

Found near Cederberg, on the west coast of South Africa, this rock art is believed to be painted by the San Bushman over 6,000 years ago.

BUSHMAN ROCK ART
SOUTH AFRICA

The Coast Salish First Nation people lived in this area for a long time before the British arrived. The date of the petroglyphs found in this park are unknown. East Sooke Park has over 50 km of hiking trails through the forest and along the coast and down to the beach.

PETROGLYPH OF A SEAL
EAST SOOKE PARK

Cuba is an island of caves, some with fantastic crystal formations including the world's tallest stalagmite at 90 meters (295 ft) high. This cave is in the Vinales region.

CAVING
CUBA

Vancouver Island has more than 1,000 caves, the highest concentration of caves in North America. One of the best places to explore them is at Horne Lake Caves Provincial Park which offers cave tours ranging from mild to wild and nearby camping, canoeing, teepees and more.

HORNE LAKE CAVES PROVINCIAL PARK
HORNE LAKE

Golf has been played at the Links at St. Andrews since the early 1400s. The course is one of the most desired destinations of many golfers.

THE OLD COURSE AT ST. ANDREWS
SCOTLAND

VICTORIA GOLF COURSE
VICTORIA

Founded in 1893, Victoria Golf Club is one of many scenic courses found on Vancouver Island. Most of the Island courses are open year-round.

Warm waters and great waves make surfing in Costa Rica very popular. Playa Grande, on the Nicoya Peninsula, is the favorite of many visitors and residents alike.

PLAYA GRANDE
COSTA RICA

LONG BEACH
TOFINO

Although the water is much cooler than Costa Rica, twenty kilometers (12.4 miles) of sandy beaches and excellent waves makes Long Beach one of Canada's best and most popular places to surf.

Sailing is very popular in this busy harbour. Avoiding the ferries and catamarans that are constantly sailing through is the biggest challenge. The annual Sydney to Hobart Yacht race starts near here.

SAILING IN SYDNEY HARBOUR
AUSTRALIA

SAILING
VICTORIA

Sailing in and around Vancouver Island is highlighted when the Swiftsure Yacht Race brings sailors from all around to participate in this annual race in May. Hundreds of boats participate in several events, sometimes including a gruelling overnight.

Also known as Lake Nicaragua, this lake near Grenada, Nicaragua is a great place to kayak and explore. Many birds and monkeys can be seen.

KAYAKING
LAKE COCIBOLCA, NICARAGUA

KAYAKING
SALISH SEA

Orcas, grey whales, seals, sea lions, sea birds, islands, bays and beaches are just some of the thrills found while kayaking around the Island.

The Swiss Alps provide numerous areas to ski. This hill near Bern has 25 runs served by 16 lifts, with the highest rising to 2,430 meters (7,972 ft).

Skiing
MEIRINGEN-HASLIGERG, SWITZERLAND

Skiing
MOUNT WASHINGTON, COMOX VALLEY

Not only does Mt. Washington have some of the best snow and ski conditions in B.C for skiing, snowboarding and tubing, it is also a summer destination for hiking and mountain biking. The summit is 1,589 meters (5,215 ft).

Antigua is the place to go for an amazing zipline "flight" over the lush tropical forest.

ZIPLINING
ANTIGUA, CARIBBEAN

ZIPLINING
VICTORIA

There are several places on the Island to soar through the air over magnificent rainforests.

Photo courtesy: Peter Berrang

When conditions are right, kite surfing and windsurfing are possible on all the Hawaiian Islands.

KITESURFING
HAWAII, U.S.A

Kitesurfing
CLOVER POINT, VICTORIA

Windsurfing and kitesurfing are popular sports around Vancouver Island. Just off the shores of Dallas Road, a few blocks from downtown Victoria, these enthusiasts have found the perfect gust of wind.

The four to five day Inca Trail hike to see the ancient Inca ruins of Machu Picchu is a very grueling task, with elevations over 3,000 meters (10,000 ft) for most of the journey—but worth every step!

Hiking
INCA TRAIL, PERU

HIKING NEAR TOFINO
PACIFIC RIM NATIONAL PARK

Hiking on Vancouver Island is endless. Forest and seaside trails are found up and down the island. From day hikes to 7 day treks along the West Coast Trail, there is something for every level of hiker.

There are 13 different species of dolphins in the waters off New Zealand. They are the fastest swimmers in the sea and often follow the bow of passing boats.

BOTTLENOSE DOLPHINS
BAY OF ISLANDS, NEW ZEALAND

Photo courtesy: Marko Khalil

PACIFIC WHITE-SIDED DOLPHINS
HECATE STRAIT (NORTH OF VANCOUVER ISLAND)

These dolphins are known for their giant leaps out of the water and can been seen doing belly-flops and somersaults. They often travel in groups of over 30. The Pacific white-sided dolphin is usually only seen in the waters to the north of the Island.

Coatis have strong limbs to climb and dig and have a reputation for intelligence like their fellow procyonid, the raccoon.

COATI
BRAZIL

Raccoons, like the deer in Victoria, can be found in many urban areas. They are very clever animals, who find their way into some unwanted places.

RACCOON
VANCOUVER ISLAND

The great blue heron is found in wetlands throughout North and Central America. This heron was found in the River Frio near the Costa Rica/Nicaragua border.

GREAT BLUE HERON
COSTA RICA

The great blue heron is just one of over 200 bird species found on the many marshes, lakes, rivers, oceans and forests of Vancouver Island.

GREAT BLUE HERON
VICTORIA

Asiatic Black Bears are also called Moon Bears, due to a white patch on their chest. This bear is at a rescue centre near Luang Probang in Laos. He was rescued from poachers who traffic in bear bile.

ASIATIC BLACK BEARS
LAOS

Vancouver Island has one of the highest densities of black bears in Canada. They can weigh over 275 kg (600 pounds) and stand 1.5 meters (5 feet) tall.

BLACK BEARS
VANCOUVER ISLAND

Lions are found mainly in Africa, with the exception of a small population in India. They are the only cats that travel in prides. All the females in the pride are related.

LIONS
SERENGETI, TANZANIA

Vancouver Island has an estimated 600 to 800 cougars, inhabiting mainly the northern part of the Island. They can also be found in some urban areas and one even found its way into the parking lot of the Empress Hotel in 1992.

COUGARS
VANCOUVER ISLAND

The South American people develop close bonds with their llamas. Most adorn their llamas with brightly coloured yarn sewn into the ear. This is not only for decoration, but also for identification.

LLAMAS
BOLIVIA

INCA
VICTORIA

"Inca" is owned by a family in Victoria. He visits seniors homes and schools and performs yearly in a Christmas Nativity play. There are many llama and alpaca farms on Vancouver Island.

There are over 500,000 Thomson Gazelles in Africa. They are fast animals that can run up to 97 kilometers per hour (60mph).

ETOSHA
NAMIBIA

UPLANDS
VICTORIA

The black-tailed deer population has exploded and many are found in urban settings throughout the Island. In some areas, residents must either fence in their flowers or expect to find them eaten by a wandering deer.

There are about 3,000 killer whales in the waters off the Norwegian and Barents Sea. During the summer months a small group of them spend time around Svalbard, the northernmost part of Norway.

ORCAS
NORWAY

ORCAS
SALISH SEA

Around 300 resident orcas, divided between the North and South Island, and 200 transient orcas swim the waters off Vancouver Island. Whale watching tours are available in many communities around the Island.